W9-DED-502

Text copyright © 2021 by Penguin Random House LLC
Cover art and interior illustrations copyright © 2021 by Åsa Gilland

All rights reserved. Published in the United States by Doubleday, an imprint of
Random House Children's Books, a division of Penguin Random House LLC, New York.

Doubleday and the colophon are registered trademarks of Penguin Random House LLC.

Visit us on the Web! rhcbooks.com

Educators and librarians, for a variety of teaching tools, visit us at RHTeachersLibrarians.com

Library of Congress Cataloging-in-Publication Data
Name: Gilland, Åsa, illustrator.
Title: Welcome to Texas / by Åsa Gilland.
Description: First edition. | New York : Doubleday, [2021] | Audience: Ages 3–7 |
Summary: "An illustrated introduction to the state of Texas" —Provided by publisher.
Identifiers: LCCN 2020009773 (print) | LCCN 2020009774 (ebook)
ISBN 978-0-593-17827-0 (hardcover) | ISBN 978-0-593-17828-7 (ebook)
Subject: LCSH: Texas—Juvenile literature
Classification: LCC F386.3 .G55 2021 (print) | LCC F386.3 (ebook) | DDC 976.4—dc23

MANUFACTURED IN CHINA
10 9 8 7 6 5 4 3 2 1
First Edition

Random House Children's Books supports the First Amendment and celebrates the right to read.

WELCOME to TEXAS

illustrated by **Åsa Gilland**

Doubleday Books for Young Readers

WELCOME to TEXAS!

WE'RE GLAD YOU'RE HERE!

ALASKA

WASHINGTON

OREGON

MONTANA

NORTH DAKOTA

MINNESOTA

WISCONSIN

MICHIGAN

IDAHO

WYOMING

SOUTH DAKOTA

NEW

CALIFORNIA

NEVADA

UTAH

COLORADO

NEBRASKA

IOWA

ILLINOIS

INDIANA

OHIO

PENNSYLVANI

WEST VIRGINIA

VIRGINI

KANSAS

MISSOURI

KENTUCKY

ARIZONA

NEW MEXICO

OKLAHOMA

ARKANSAS

TENNESSEE

NORTH CAROLINA

SOUTH CAROLINA

HAWAII

TEXAS

AUSTIN

MISSISSIPPI

LOUISIANA

ALABAMA

GEORGIA

FLORIDA

MAINE

NEW HAMPSHIRE
MASSACHUSETTS
RHODE ISLAND
CONNECTICUT
JERSEY
ARE
ND

Capital city: Austin
State nickname: The Lone Star State
State motto: "Friendship"

TEXAS is BIG!

It's the second-largest state in the USA. It has big ranches, big farms, big forests, and big cities.

The word "Texas" comes from the Native American Caddo people, who were among the first to live on this land. The Caddo word "taysha" means "friend."

AMARILLO

LUBBOCK

EL PASO

RIO GRANDE

FORT WORTH-

PLANO-

-DALLAS

-ARLINGTON

AUSTIN

UNITED STATES

UNITED STATES

HOUSTON

SAN ANTONIO

CORPUS CHRISTI

LAREDO

A big state like Texas needs THREE official state mammals!

Can you guess how the Texas longhorn got its name?
The horns on these cattle can grow as long as ten feet across!

NINE-BANDED ARMADILLO

This clever creature keeps safe with its armor of hard scales. It finds insects to eat by burying its snout in the ground.

MEXICAN FREE-TAILED BAT

In Austin from spring to early fall, you can see Mexican free-tailed bats flying from under the Congress Avenue Bridge when the sun is setting. How many are there? 1.5 million!

The state bird of Texas is the mockingbird. It loves to chirp and tweet, and it even sings the songs of other birds and animals!

But don't let that pretty song fool you. It's also a fierce fighter. If an animal or person gets near its nest, the mockingbird will swoop down fast to scare the intruder away.

The state flower of Texas is the bluebonnet. It got its name because its petals look like bonnets, which pioneer women in Texas used to wear to keep the hot sun off their heads.

BLUEBONNET

TEXAS STATE FLOWER

WILLIAM B. TRAVIS
COMMANDER OF THE
REPUBLIC OF TEXAS

You might hear Texans say "Remember the Alamo!" They are talking about a famous battle in San Antonio, when Texans fought to make Texas a separate country. You can still go to the Alamo today!

Texas was its own country for ten years. In 1845, it joined the United States.

GENERAL ANTONIO LÓPEZ DE SANTA ANNA OF THE MEXICAN REPUBLIC

Mexico is just across the border from Texas,
and many Mexican people call Texas home.

On Christmas Eve, it is traditional for Mexican families in Texas to make and eat tamales, which are corn husks filled with cornmeal dough, meat, cheese, or vegetables.
¡Feliz Navidad!

Texans love food! Luckily, Texas is a state with lots of good things to eat!

CHILI

PICKLED JALAPEÑO SLICES

TACOS

HAMBURGERS

QUESO

BARBECUE

CHICKEN-FRIED STEA

Texans also love football! In cities and towns across the state, fans gather on Friday nights to watch high school games. Go, team!

Would you like to meet a real cowboy or cowgirl?
You can at RodeoHouston!

At the livestock show, watch cows being milked, honeybees buzzing in a hive, and chicks hatching from eggs! Grab your cowboy boots and hat, and let's go!

A big place like Texas has a lot of unusual things to see if you're out for a drive:

CADILLAC RANCH

Are those cars growing out of the ground? Artists created this strange ranch in Amarillo by burying ten Cadillacs nose-down. Visitors from all over the world have painted the cars bright colors.

BIG TEX

Look way up and say howdy to Big Tex, a fifty-five-foot-high cowboy who towers over the State Fair of Texas, in Dallas.

MS. PEARL
THE GIANT SQUIRREL

Cedar Creek is home to Ms. Pearl, the world's tallest squirrel statue. Why is she holding a giant pecan? Nearby is a vending machine that sells freshly baked pecan pies!

If you love Texas, then you're a Texas kid!
And Texas kids are the best!

UNITED STATES
AME